OLD CHINA
IN HISTORIC PHOTOGRAPHS

288 VIEWS BY
Ernst Boerschmann

With a New Introduction by Wan-go Weng

Dover Publications, Inc. New York

FRONTISPIECE: Ming Dynasty memorial gate (pai lou) in Yanzhou xian [Yenchoufu], Shandong sheng [Shantung Province]. (See Introduction.)

Published in Canada by General Publishing Company, Ltd., 30 Lesmill Road, Don Mills, Toronto, Ontario.
Published in the United Kingdom by Constable and Company, Ltd., 10 Orange Street, London WC2H 7EG.

This Dover edition, first published in 1982, is a revised republication of *Picturesque China / Architecture and Landscape / A Journey Through Twelve Provinces,* as published by Brentano's, New York, n.d. (a translation, by Louis Hamilton, of a work originally published in German by Ernst Wasmuth, Berlin, n.d.). See the Publisher's Note on the opposite page for a full description of the revision that has been undertaken.

Manufactured in the United States of America
Dover Publications, Inc.
180 Varick Street
New York, N.Y. 10014

Library of Congress Cataloging in Publication Data

Boerschmann, Ernst, 1873–1949.
    Old China in historic photographs.

    Translation of: Baukunst und Landschaft in China.
    1. China—Description and travel—1901–1948—
Views. 2. Architecture—China. I. Title.
DS710.B65913 1982   779′.9915.1043   81-17322
ISBN 0-486-24282-X   AACR2

PUBLISHER'S NOTE, 1982

WHEN the skillful and sensitive photographer Ernst Boerschmann (1873–1949) photographed China during his sojourn there between 1906 and 1909, his attitude was not that of a reporter or ethnographer. He was seeking out the timeless sites of local religion and legend, especially as embodied in ecclesiastical and traditional architecture and in the setting of such architecture within the landscape, exemplifying man's oneness with nature.

The original edition of this book, *Picturesque China,* contained 288 of Boerschmann's photos. All of them are included in the present revision, but their sequence has been drastically altered. Although the original edition showed signs of following a rational plan, photos of one and the same province, one and the same city and even one and the same monument often appeared at unusually wide and erratic intervals. The present edition not only reunites like items, but also adopts totally the order in which localities are described in the comprehensive Nagel guide to China (Geneva; the 1967 edition was used). This has been done for the convenience of readers desirous of finding further information readily. (The villages and other small sites photographed by Boerschmann and not included in Nagel have been placed near the closest respective sites in Nagel).

Another serious shortcoming of the original edition was the dispersal of information between the captions and the List of Illustrations. In the present edition the totally revised captions contain all of this information in addition to various other data culled from Nagel or furnished by Mr. Wan-go Weng (see below for his contributions). The old List of Illustrations (as well as the old Index of Names and Groups) has been omitted. The new List of Photographs serves merely as a handy listing of the pictures, which makes the groupings by province and smaller subdivisions instantly clear.

Chinese proper names are given in the modern *pinyin* transcription system, which was developed in mainland China in recent years and is now being adopted in all forward-looking and scholarly publications. On the first appearance of each *pinyin* term, an older form (or forms) is supplied within square brackets, usually in the spelling that was employed in the original edition of this book, which was a modification of the old Wade-Giles transcription scheme. Generally speaking, if the Chinese name of a site or monument is given in *pinyin,* the inference can be drawn that it still exists (at least to some extent) and is described in Nagel; if only an old form in brackets is given, the opposite inference can generally be drawn. Much more explicit information about the survival or nonsurvival of many monuments is furnished in the new Introduction (see below).

The map of China has been completely revised to supply *pinyin* forms of the localities.

Boerschmann's original introductory essay, which told almost nothing about his travels but concentrated on a subjective and at times unscientific interpretation of Chinese philosophy and culture, has been omitted here. In place of this, it has been our good fortune to obtain from Mr. Wan-go Weng, a distinguished historian of Chinese art and culture, a new Introduction that places Boerschmann's sojourn within its historical context and then goes on to outline the events and forces that have extensively changed the face of the country since Boerschmann's day. Mr. Weng then goes on to give accurate, up-to-date information about the present condition of scores of sites included in the book—invaluable indications that cannot readily be found elsewhere. Although Mr. Weng's name appears only on the Introduction, his efforts have also enriched our captions, since he also supplied the correct *pinyin* for many of the sites included and—most significantly—pointed out the current designations of numerous places that have undergone a total name change, making it possible to identify them in Nagel and other current literature.

CHINA

1 Beijing
2 Great Wall (only the parts near Beijing are shown)
3 Chengde
4 Xi ling
5 Luan River
6 Jinan
7 Tai shan
8 Qufu / Yanzhou
9 Taiyuan / Yangwuzhen
10 Wutai shan
11 Linfen / Mengcheng
12 Yuncheng
13 Xi'an
14 Hua shan
15 Qinling shan

16 Suzhou
17 Shanghai
18 Hangzhou / Haining
19 Ningbo / Tiantongsi
20 Putuo
21 Yichang
22 Changsha / Liling
23 Heng shan / Hengyang
24 Lake Dongting, or Dongting hu
25 Sanduao
26 Fuzhou
27 Guangzhou
28 Wuzhou
29 Guilin / Pingle
30 Chengdu
31 Shibaozhai / Wan xian

32 Chongqing
33 Guan xian / Qingcheng shan / Fengdu
34 Yibin / Leshan
35 Emei shan
36 Luzhou / Ziliujing
37 Guangyuan
38 Fengjie
39 Ya'an

Only localities mentioned in the text are indicated on this map. Only main centers are shown, not nearby villages, monasteries or countryside. The long dotted line is the course of the Chang jiang (Yangzi River).

Introduction to the Dover Edition

BY WAN-GO WENG

I

ONE year after Dr. Sun Yat-sen formed the United League (Tongmenghui) in Tokyo to coordinate diverse revolutionary elements inside and outside China for the overthrow of Manchu imperial rule, a German photographer named Ernst Boerschmann came to the dying empire searching for the picturesque, the mysterious and the imperishable. The time was 1906, during which the Qing (Manchu) court sent five special envoys to Western nations and Japan to seek the new and powerful and unlock the secret of Japan's strength which had defeated Czarist Russia. Boerschmann left China in 1909, the first year of the reign of the child emperor Puyi under his father's regency. That the Qing envoys learned nothing from their quest is history, for by 1911 Sun Yat-sen succeeded in staging an armed revolution which ended the imperial era in China; what the photographer reaped from his three-year, twelve-province journey was a collection of excellent pictures edited into this book.

II

To understand the collective and individual value of these pictures and appreciate their significance, one must obtain at least a brief view of the tumultuous events that have occurred between Boerschmann's journey and the present day. Numerous local insurrections broke out in the last years of Qing rule, mostly in the central and southern provinces. The revolt escalated in tempo and magnitude until, in October of 1911, the Wuchang Uprising signaled a national revolution. But no sooner had Sun Yat-sen become the first president of the new republic than Yuan Shikai, the top general of the defeated imperial house, snatched away his triumph.

Yuan forced Sun to retire so that he could take over the presidency in preparation for realizing his ultimate ambition—to install himself on the throne as founding emperor of a new dynasty. This he did in December 1915, provoking throughout the land denunciations so overwhelming as to cause his collapse and death within a few months. It was hardly surprising, for ever since the irrational outburst against foreign encroachment, known as the Boxer Rebellion, convulsed the nation in 1900, China's central control had been disintegrating. As revolution and counterrevolution raged from 1911 onward, chaotic internal strife among warlords took over. Greedy and callous generals with regional power bases vied with each other for supremacy, shifting capriciously from alliance to war and making the whole of China, except for a few pockets of foreign concessions in cities like Tianjin [T'ientsin] and Shanghai, into a battleground.

Meantime, the First World War provided Japan with an opportunity to demand special privileges, since the Western powers were busily locked in their life-and-death struggle. The survival of the Chinese nation was at stake, and intense feelings against feudalism as well as foreign domination came to a head in 1919 when the

May Fourth Movement, spearheaded by 3000 Peking students, marked the beginning of the second phase of revolution, which was soon joined by workers and merchants in Shanghai, Tianjin, Nanjing [Nanking], Hangzhou and many other major cities.

July 1, 1921 saw the birth of the Chinese Communist Party. It joined forces with Chiang Kai-shek's Nationalist army in the Northern Expedition of 1926 to 1927 against warlords. The success of this Expedition and the subsequent purging of the Communists in April 1927 established Chiang Kai-shek as the dominant force. By 1928, the Nationalist flag flew over Manchuria as well as the rest of China. In 1930, Chiang initiated "Bandit Extermination" campaigns against the Communist base in Jiangxi [Kiangsi] province; however, his last and greatest campaign of 1934 failed to stop the "Long March" of the Red guerrillas escaping from his iron grip. The surviving marchers reestablished themselves in the northwestern wasteland.

While Chiang's armies concentrated on waging a civil war, Japan created the Mukden Incident in 1931 and promptly occupied Manchuria, installing the last Qing emperor Puyi as the puppet ruler of her new colony Manchukuo. The next step for the ambitious invader was to set up a buffer zone in North China, undermining Nationalist authority over that critical area. In 1937, Japan took the third and final step: her forces attacked the Marco Polo Bridge near Peking and then Shanghai, spreading a war of conquest with the whole of China as the ultimate prize. Now the ancient land once again became a huge battlefield, and Japanese bombers struck cities and countryside at will, concentrating their fury on the Chinese wartime capital Chongqing in the hinterland. Behind the fluid battle lines, the Nationalists and the Communists cooperated on the surface against their common enemy but the alliance was disrupted in 1941 and civil war resumed in 1945 upon Japan's surrender.

In 1946, scattered armed conflicts burst into a full-scale war and in the next two years the Communists staged decisive battles in Manchuria, North, Northwest and Central China, routing Nationalist armies. By 1949, Mao Zedong's [Tse-tung] party established the People's Republic with its capital at Peking, or Beijing, and Chiang Kai-shek retreated to Canton—and Taiwan soon after. So, at the halfway mark of our century, the war on China's home ground was finally over.

So it seemed.

III

In spite of China's involvement in the Korean War in October 1950, the kind of peace that her people had not known for many decades prevailed. By 1961, the government announced the first list of 180 "Protected National Important Cultural Relics" of great historical, artistic and scientific value, including 33 sites and buildings in memory of the revolution, 14 cave temples, 77 ancient works of architecture and monuments, 11 groups or individual pieces of stone engravings and other types of sculptures, 26 archaeological sites and 19 major tombs and tomb grounds. Such cultural "units" immediately enjoyed maintenance and restoration with the help of the national budget and manpower, and the list was to be expanded from time to time. On provincial and local levels, comparatively minor sites, buildings and cultural objects were to be recognized and protected accordingly.

But the thunder of destruction struck again in 1966. The Red Guards went on a rampage under the banner of "Cultural Revolution" to eradicate the "degenerate," "corrupt" and "poisonous" past. Their youthful energies were unleashed to attack anything old, bourgeois or foreign, targeting ancient buildings and cultural relics as fair game for mindless vandalism. The nation, and indeed the world, owe eternal gratitude to the then premier Zhou [Chou] Enlai, who tirelessly directed efforts to protect as many important sites and objects as possible, and to courageous local individuals and groups who risked their lives to counter the blind forces masquerading as spearheads of progress. Not until 1976, after the death of Mao Zedong and the downfall of the "Gang of Four," did calm and order return to a tortured land and its ancient culture.

From the brief account above, it is evident that the chance for survival was slim indeed for what Boerschmann saw and photographed some 70 years ago. The unrelenting eraser of time alone, with its abrasive winds, water, lightning and earthquakes, could have reduced all man's work to nature if man did not try to preserve them; but man's worst enemy—himself—hastened the process with misuse, vandalism and, above all, war. Even well-intentioned but ill-advised restorations have contributed in some cases to converting treasures into trash. So the marvel is that, of the 288 pictures in this book, roughly half still reflect the current appearance of their subjects, giving us the impression that China, after all, is quite imperishable. For the other half of the book, alas, the pictures have become truly historical; they are the previous images of a China that has gone forever.

IV

Among the vanished sights there are three broad categories: (1) works of architecture and objects that have been destroyed or severely damaged beyond restoration; (2) landscapes that remain largely the same but are now covered with different buildings and vegetation; and (3) people who no longer look the same or do the same things depicted in the photographs. Interesting cases in each category will serve as examples, with their page numbers given in italics.

In the first category, the degree of change varies from instance to instance, ranging from total disappearance to extensive replacement.

a. Gates and Walls:

1: Beijing. Part of the city walls. All the walls around the city have been eliminated; left standing are only a few corner towers and major gates. Camel caravans are a vanished sight. Another city shorn of its walls is Canton, now called Guangzhou; hence the view in *186* is also a memory.

2: Beijing. Southern approach to the Imperial Palace. Everything in front of the double-roofed building in the background, which is the beautifully renovated gate called Tian'anmen, has been razed to make room for the vast Tian'anmen Square. The central three-doored structure in the middle ground was Zhonghuamen, another gate on the north-south axis leading to the Forbidden City. In the original edition, Boerschmann misnamed the picture "Imperial Palace."

b. Religious Edifices:

29: Beijing area. Door in the Temple of the Wind God. Chinese history records several major religious persecutions when temples and images were smashed, defiled or appropriated for secular use. It is uncertain whether the examples cited in this section were victims of the latest persecution, the Cultural Revolution, or succumbed long ago under various circumstances, including neglect and abuse. This Temple of the Wind God is gone, as are the pass temple on the road to Jehol (*30*) and the unusual Cave Monastery of the Cloud Summit (*73*). The monastery buildings on the Golden Summit of Emei shan (*243–248*) went up in flames; the altars and interior furnishings in the Monastery of the Celestial Boy near Ningbo (*130 & 131*) have vanished, though the much-changed buildings still exist. Of course, the monks going to prayers (*133*) and the abbot and his staff (*132*) died many years ago, leaving only these rare photographs.

ix

c. Burial Places:

25: Entrance to a cemetery in the Plain of Beijing. As a rule, private burial grounds have been leveled in the past few decades; during the Cultural Revolution, they were prime targets for elimination. The following pictures all belong to this group: *129, 168–171, 190–193, 210, 267, 268 & 285.* Boerschmann seemed to be fascinated by these private tombs in the countryside, and most of his selections tend to be elaborately decorated in the late "Chinese Rococo" style of dubious artistic merit. Nevertheless, they did represent a kind of Chinese folk art and the best of them deserved preservation, in pictures if not in actuality.

287: Tomb pagoda in the Golden Summit Monastery, Ya'an. Another kind of burial was the small stone pagoda or other types of structures for housing the remains of high monks; many of them suffered the same fate as secular cemeteries. This one, together with those in *136, 139* and *286,* was destroyed. Among the exceptions is the Buddhist cemetery in the Monastery of the Magical Cliff (*52*), which escaped annihilation.

64: Gate on the way to the Tomb of Confucius, Qufu. Second only in importance to imperial tombs are the burial places of great figures in Chinese history, Confucius and Yue Fei being the two included in this book. Confucius, considered the most influential thinker and teacher in the old society, had been an object of vilification since 1919 and the intensity of attack reached a crescendo in the Cultural Revolution. Yet efforts to defend him and his teachings were equally stubborn, for much of his philosophy is still relevant and his historical position remains unshaken. Although this gate to his grave was severely damaged and parts of the stone stele were smashed, his tomb and his temple in the same town (*63*) survived the ordeal. As a matter of fact, Confucian temples in many cities were appropriated for other uses—the marvelous Xi'an Provincial Museum being a prime example. However, the ones pictured in *231* and *260–262* have most likely disappeared, and the very elaborate edifice in *149* is gone.

116: The tomb of Yue Fei in Hangzhou was wrecked during the Cultural Revolution but recently rebuilt. General Yue, a twelfth-century patriot who defended the Southern Song regime successfully against the northern Tartars, met his early and tragic death at the hands of court traitors who executed him for insubordination. Mourned and loved by the people for centuries, he became a symbol of absolute loyalty to emperor and country.

d. Memorial Gates, Family Temples and Provincial Clubs:

Independent of but associated with cemeteries are memorial gates, erected to honor the brave, the loyal, the filial and the chaste. Being symbolic structures that extol feudalistic virtues, many were dismantled or defaced. *157, 198, 208, 251* and the Frontispiece belong to this group. Memorial altars and temples should be similarly classified; the images in *156, 211, 215* and *250* are visions of the past.

164: Family temple in the southern part of Hunan. The family was the foundation of old Chinese society (and I believe it still is) and the family temple its conspicuous representation. Besides housing tablets honoring one's ancestors on its altars, the temple also served as a meeting place for clan affairs and the temporary care center for needy members. The fancy structure in this picture and another in *155* became natural targets under campaigns to wipe out the old. An extension of such family organizations was the local or provincial clubs where people hailing from the same town or province met. Many of these temples and clubs can no longer be found; thus the fate of the Fujian Club (*122–124*) in Ningbo is dubious. Some were defaced outside and gutted inside, but a few have luckily been repaired and transformed into new institutional buildings: the Shanxi Club in Ziliujing (*255–258*) has become a museum for the salt industry, and the ancestral temple of the Chen family in Canton (*180–182*) has been under extensive repair for conversion into an art gallery.

For the second category of change, vanishing landscapes, this book provides many nostalgic scenes of a China that was.

49 & 50: Lake of the Great Brightness in Jinan—the site remains the same, but the architecture has changed.

214: Village of Hanzhou—this serene scenery is no more.

222–224: The Min River suspension bridge at Guan xian has been replaced by one of steel and concrete, as has the one over the Ya River (*284*).

276: Leshan xian—no longer the same houses and foliage. A modern bridge of steel now spans the Min River.

Of all these other Sichuan sites—Qionglai xian (*274*), Qingcheng shan typical scene (*240*), countryside between Luzhou and Ziliujing (*249*), salt boats in the industrial district of Ziliujing (*253 & 254*), narrow streets in Chongqing (*218 & 219*), Fengjie xian (*277*) and Shibaozhai (*217*)—only the pagoda clinging to the rock in *217* still exists.

Casualties in other provinces: the bridge in Liling (*154*) and Hengyang shi (*160*), both in Hunan; the scenes of Guilin (*199 & 200*) in Guangxi. In Guangdong: in no. *187*, the five-storied tower at the left still exists but the wall, the temple and the mosque are gone. Also no longer the same are the Fuzhou harbor (*167*) and the view of Sanduao (*166*), both in Fujian. In the view of West Lake near Hangzhou, in Zhejiang, the Thunder Cliff Pagoda collapsed from disrepair in the 1920s. Along the shores of the West Lake (see also *114*), much building is taking place to meet the demands of blooming tourism. The picture-book perfect scene of the south wall of Ningbo, in the same province, is, alas, just a page out of this picture book!

Of the third category, people and activities belonging to another era, we have the following examples:

26 & 27: North Chinese traveling carts on the Plain of Beijing—animal power is still commonly relied upon in China, though the carts now sport rubber tires and are used mostly for carrying goods, not people (as in these neatly covered vehicles).

74 & 75: Journeying to Wutai shan—a team of pack mules or donkeys with attendant coolies was essential for the Chinese safari; today Chinese-made jeeps would be employed to negotiate this kind of terrain.

216: Waterwheel at Luojiang—waterwheels still help farmers in many localities, but sedan chairs such as the one carried by men in the right-hand corner of the picture disappeared quite some time ago. The same comment applies to *209*, a journey in Guangxi Province.

V

At this juncture, we should look at the other half of the picture—that is, those cultural relics that have survived and are in good condition. A transitional case is the Empress Wu memorial temple at Guangyuan xian (*270 & 271*). Together with the Thousand Buddha Rock on the opposite bank of the river (*272 & 273*), it was endangered by the construction of a highway and railroad in the 1930s when the Nationalists ruled. As a matter of fact, the southern end of the Thousand Buddha

Rock was dynamited, blasting away several hundred caves and niches of Buddhist images. The same engineering projects cleared out two temple halls for roadbeds, fortunately sparing the major part of the Rock and Empress Wu's edifice, which has a cave temple of its own above the buildings. Today these monuments are under the protection of the National Important Cultural Relics Act.

Altogether there are 23 such protected units in this book (see the complete list in note 2 to this introduction), including the following notable items on the must-see list of present-day tourists in Beijing: the Forbidden City (Imperial Palace), seen in the distance in *2;* sections of the Great Wall (*19*); the Temple of Heaven (*3 & 4*); the Ming Tombs (*20); the Western Tombs of the Qing imperial house (*40–46*); and the Summer Palace (*9*).

The summer residence of the Qing emperors, with lama monasteries, in Jehol (*31–39*) was recently opened to the public; extensive restoration, which may continue for years, has recovered some of the atmosphere of bygone days. In the 1920s, dozens of beautiful structures were brutally dismantled by a warlord stationed here whose unruly troops pulled down the pillars with teams of horses. It is beyond the means of the government now to recreate the glory of Emperor Qianlong, who reigned from 1736 to 1796 and was mainly responsible for the development of this capital away from the capital.

Probably even greater in scale and requiring an incredible amount of rescuing is the group of monasteries in the high valley of Wutai shan (*76–85*). According to a 1980 report, 47 monasteries are now standing, including the oldest extant wooden structure in China, the hall of Nanchansi or Temple of Southern Chan Buddhism, built in 782, and the second oldest—but much larger—hall of Fuoguangsi or Temple of Buddha's Light, built in 857. Both, of course, are on the list for protection. In the grand view of *76,* the temple in the foreground is now in disrepair, but the great white pagoda, the centerpiece of the whole complex (close up in *85*), looks none the worse for wear. Also in good condition is the major building of Xiantongsi (*80*), the interior space of which is free of pillars and beams and has long been admired as an architectural wonder.

VI

Universal respect for the nation's cultural heritage, dictated by a complex of reasons ranging from nostalgia, aesthetics and pride to consideration of the monuments as commercial assets for tourism, has persisted in China throughout one of her most turbulent periods in history. An official protective policy dating to 1961, carried out despite personal dangers by dedicated men and women in all corners of the land, has stood the acid test of the disastrous decade (1966–76) of Cultural Revolution which was unabashedly anti-culture. Accomplished works of preservation and restoration over an area as large as China can only be uneven, from magnificent to barely acceptable. It would be most interesting for the reader on tour to compare what Boerschmann saw with current actuality. One should not be surprised by the inescapable imprint of time as represented by the period style of modern restorers and craftsmen, whose taste in color and pattern as well as choice of materials tend to be lacking in subtlety. The laudable open-to-the public policy fails to cope with population explosion and public ignorance, making one wonder how much abuse a stone elephant or Buddha, a bronze lion or incense burner, an ancient tree or delicate balustrade can take from youthful climbers and not-so-youthful graffiti inscribers. A case in point is the marble stairs and brick floors yielding to millions of footsteps in the Forbidden City, which houses the Palace Museum. Peace and limited prosperity have enabled thousands of people to trek here and gaze at an unbeatable artistic complex—comparable to a combination of the treasures in the Louvre and the architectural splendor of Versailles—seven days a week, 365 days a year. Industrialization and urbanization have further brought corrosive fumes to wear down glazed tiles and painted pillars, bronze sculpture and stone carvings. The urgent need for saving endangered cultural relics through education and training of more administrative and technical personnel and meaningful coordination among architects, archaeologists, art historians, engineers, craftsmen and conservation experts, and above all, love and care from a knowledgeable and disciplined public, can no longer be ignored. A movement for courteous behavior and aesthetic appreciation has been launched and on its success rests the hope that that part of the pictures in this book which still can be measured against reality will not become merely historical.

NOTES

1. During the past two years, I traveled through half of the provinces covered by Boerschmann, in addition to several others that he did not visit. I saw more than a score of the sites that he photographed. For information on the majority of the places that I have not personally inspected, I relied upon the first-hand knowledge of Mr. Wang Shixiang and Mr. Luo Zhewen, both of the State Administrative Bureau of Museums and Archaeological Data in Beijing, and Mr. Chai Zejun of the Research Institute of Ancient Architecture in Taiyuan. I take this opportunity to acknowledge my indebtedness to their generous help. Opinions expressed in this essay, of course, remain my own.

2. The 23 units on the 1961 list of "National Important Cultural Relics" included in this book are: (1) page 2, List No. 100; (2) pages 3 & 4, List No. 105; (3) page 5, List No. 75; (4) page 9, List No. 122; (5) page 19, List No. 101; (6) page 20, List No. 178; (7) pages 31 & 32, List No. 116; (8) pages 33–35 & 37, List No. 117; (9) pages 36 & 38, List No. 118; (10) page 39, List No. 123; (11) page 40, List No. 180; (12) page 63, List No. 99; (13) page 64, List No. 163; (14) page 71, List No. 85; (15 & 16) two temples shown on page 76, List Nos. 79 & 80; (17) page 93, List No. 104; (18) page 97, List No. 64; (19) page 98, List No. 63; (20) page 116, List No. 176; (21) page 243 (bronze and iron sculptures), List No. 133; (22) pages 270 & 271, List No. 43; (23) pages 272 & 273, List No. 44.

LIST OF PHOTOGRAPHS

FRONTISPIECE: Yanzhou xian, Shandong sheng [Shantung Province], memorial gate

BEIJING [PEKING] and HEBEI SHENG [CHIHLI PROVINCE]

Beijing and Environs

PAGE
1. Part of city walls
2. Southern approach to Imperial Palace
3 & 4. Temple of Heaven
5. Temple of Five Pagodas
6 & 7. Temple of Celestial Peace
8. Yellow Temple
9. Summer Palace grounds
10–17. Temple of Azure Clouds
18. Qingyiyuan
19. Great Wall of China
20. Ming Dynasty imperial tombs
21 & 22. Pagoda at Balizhuang
23. Temple of the Terrace of Initiation
24. Monastery garden
25. Entrance to a cemetery
26 & 27. Traveling carts
28. Tongzhou canal
29. Temple of the Wind God
30. Pass temple on the road to Chengde

Chengde [Jehol]

31 & 32. Temple of Universal Joy
33 & 34. Potala
35–38. Views in a lamasery
39. Bridge in the imperial park

Other Sites

40–46. Western Tombs of the Manchu Dynasty emperors
47 & 48. Luan River

SHANDONG SHENG [SHANTUNG PROVINCE]

49 & 50. Jinan: Lake of the Great Brightness
51–54. Monastery of the Magical Cliff
55 & 56. Qingyangshu: Temple of the Tai Shan Goddess
57–59. Tai Shan Temple
60–62. Tai shan views
63 & 64. Qufu: Temple of Confucius & gate
65 & 66. Yanzhou xian: gate & bridge

SHANXI SHENG [SHANSI PROVINCE]

67–70. Taiyuan: Temple of Great Mercy & other views

71 & 72. Jinci temple complex
73. Mian shan: Monastery of the Cloud Summit
74 & 75. Traveling to Wutai shan
76–85. Wutai shan: views & details of monasteries
86–88. Linfen: defiles in loess & Emperor Yao temple
89. Mengcheng: Emperor Huangdi memorial hall
90 & 91. Yunchen xian: salt lake & image of Guandi
92. Yangwuzhen: residence

SHAANXI SHENG [SHENSI PROVINCE]

93–98. Xi'an: North Gate, Great Mosque, Goose Pagodas
99–102. Hua shan: views & great temple
103. Mian xian: image of Ma Chao
104–109. Qin ling shan: details of temples & monasteries

JIANGSU SHENG [KIANGSU PROVINCE] and SHANGHAI

110. Suzhou: thousand-armed Guanyin
111 & 112. Shanghai: pagoda & residence

ZHEJIANG SHENG [CHEKIANG PROVINCE]

Hangzhou and Vicinity

113 & 114. West Lake
115. Monastery of the Holy Succession
116. Tomb of General Yue Fei
117. Refuge of Souls Valley
118. Temple of the Forest of Clouds
119. Imperial Library
120. Haining: bore at mouth of Qiantang River

Ningbo and Tiantongsi

121. South wall of city
122–124. Fujian Club
125. Temple entrances
126 & 127. Stores
128 & 129. Countryside between Ningbo & Tiantongsi
130–133. Tiantongsi: Monastery of the Celestial Boy

Putuo

134. General view
135. Pagoda of Prince Buddha
136. Priest's grave
137–144. Monastery of the Rain of Law

Yichang

145. Brush Holder Mountain
146 & 147. Temple of the Dragon King
148. Entrance to a temple

HUNAN SHENG [PROVINCE]

Changsha
149. Great Temple of Confucius
150 & 151. Ancestral temple of the Chen family
152. Temple of Zuo Wenxiang
153. Temple of the god of literature

Other Sites
154–157. Liling: bridge, memorial temple & gates
158 & 159. Heng shan: great temple
160 & 161. Hengyang shi: temple & street
162 & 163. Lake Dongting
164 & 165. Views in southern Hunan

FUJIAN SHENG [FUKIEN PROVINCE]

166. San du ao

Fuzhou and Environs
167. Harbor with Drum Mountain
168–171. Graves
172–177. Monastery of the Boiling Spring

GUANGDONG SHENG [CANTON; KUANGTUNG PROVINCE]

Guangzhou and Environs
178 & 179. Great Mosque
180–182. Ancestral temple of the Chen family
183–185. Temple of the God of medicine
186–188. North hill
189. Monastery of the Sea Banner
190–195. White Cloud Mountain & the monastery Nengrensi

GUANGXI SHENG [KUANGSI PROVINCE]

196–198. Wuzhou: bronze censers & memorial gate
199–204. Guilin: general views, pagoda, bridge, Fuzhou Club
205. Pingle xian
206 & 207. Gui River
208–211. Views in the countryside

SICHUAN SHENG [SZECH'UAN PROVINCE]

Chengdu and Environs
212. Hall of Laozi in a Taoist monastery
213. Wenshu Monastery
214–216. Villages in the plain of Chengdu

217. Shibaozhai & the Rock of the Ten Thousand Shadows
218–221. Chongqing: streets & cave temple

Guan xian
222. General view
223 & 224. Suspension bridge
225–230. Temple of Li Bing & Erlang
231. Temple of Confucius
232 & 233. Temple of the Tamed Dragon
234. Guanyin grotto in the Soul Cliff
235. View down Min River

Qingcheng shan
236. Cave of the Morning Sun
237. Rock chapel
238. Main hall of a monastery
239. Hall of the Celestial Queen
240. Typical scene
241 & 242. Yibin: general view & monastery

Emei shan
243. Monastery of Ten Thousand Years
244. Golden Summit
245–247. Monasteries on the Golden Summit
248. Hermitage of Pure Sound

Ziliujing and Environs
249–251. Countryside between Luzhou & Ziliujing
252. Nanhuagong
253 & 254. Salt-well industrial district
255–258. Shanxi Club
259. Yuntan

Wan xian and Environs
260–262. Temple of Confucius
263. Temple of Lord Chen
264–266. Temple of General Zhang Fei
267 & 268. Mountain of the Sedan-Chair Knob
269. Gate of a fortified village

Other Sites
270–273. Guangyuan xian: Empress Wu temple & rock Buddhas
274. Qionglai xian
275. Fengdu
276. Leshan xian
277. Fengjie xian
278–281. Bellows Gorge
282–287. Ya'an: views & Golden Summit Monastery

Beijing [Peking; Peiching]. Part of the city walls, originally built early 15th century. (See Introduction.)

Beijing. Southern approach to the Imperial Palace (now Tian'anmen Square). (See Introduction.)

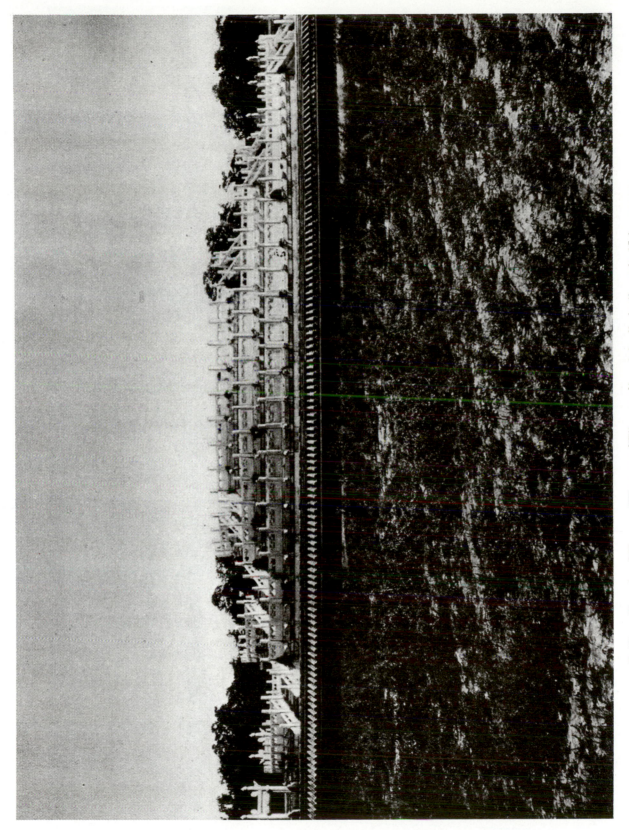

Beijing. Temple of Heaven (Tian tan [T'ien tan]), originally built early 15th century. Terrace of Sacrifices. (See Introduction.)

Beijing. Temple of Heaven. Hall of Annual Prayers. (See Introduction.)

Beijing suburbs. Five-towered structure in the Temple of Five Pagodas (Wutasi [Wu t'a sze]), 1473.

Beijing suburbs. Temple of Celestial Peace (Tianningsi [T'ien ning sze]). Pagoda, early 12th century.

Beijing suburbs. Temple of Celestial Peace. Part of the base of the pagoda.

Beijing suburbs. Marble stupa in the lamasery of the Yellow Temple (Huangsi [Huang sze]), ca. 1780.

Beijing environs. End of a bridge in the grounds of the Summer Palace. (See Introduction.)

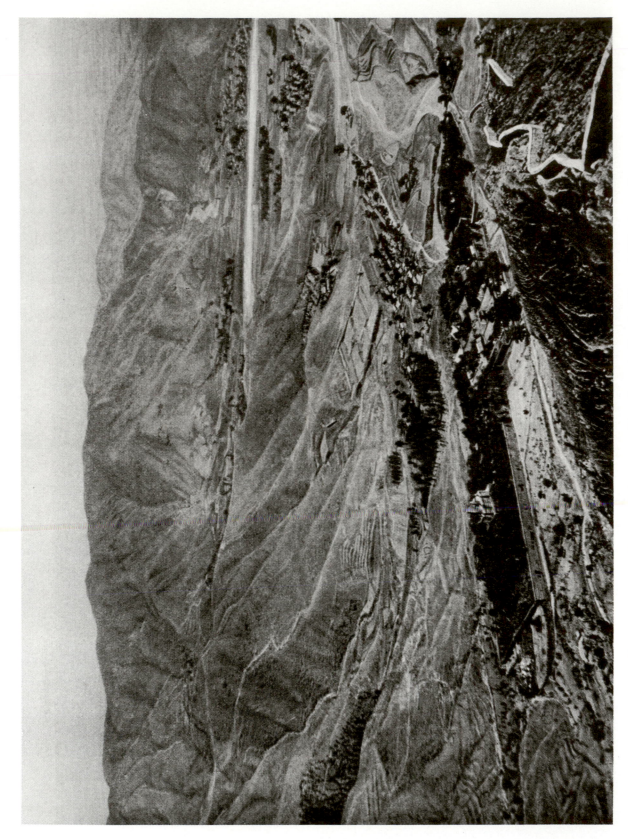

Beijing environs. Temple of Azure (or Blue-Green) Clouds (Biyunsi [Pi yün sze]), founded ca. 1330, in the Fragrant Hills (Xiang shan) [Western Hills (Si shan)].

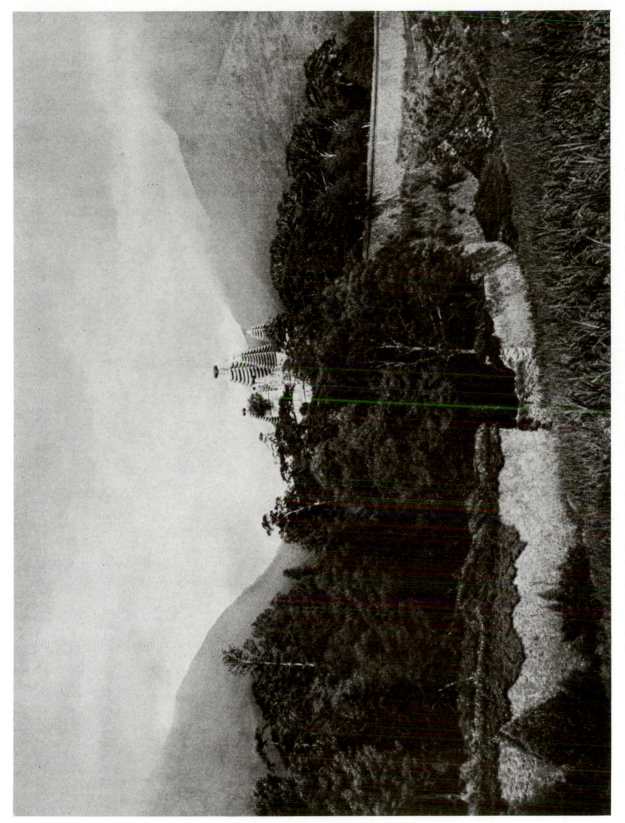

Beijing environs. Temple of Azure Clouds. Marble pagoda (Pagoda of the Diamond Throne), 1748.

Beijing environs. Temple of Azure Clouds. Staircase to the pagoda.

Beijing environs. Temple of Azure Clouds. Back view of the pagoda, seen through white-barked pines.

Beijing environs. Temple of Azure Clouds. Detail of the Pagoda.

Beijing environs. Temple of Azure Clouds. Topmost platform of the pagoda.

Beijing environs. Temple of Azure Clouds. Lamaist goddess, detail of the pagoda.

Beijing environs. Temple of Azure Clouds. Bodhisattva, detail of the pagoda.

Beijing environs. Colored glazed gate at Qingyiyuan [Ts'ing i yüan] in the Fragrant Hills.

Great Wall of China (Wan li chang cheng [Wan li ch'ang ch'eng], "the wall 10,000 *li* long"). (See Introduction.)

Road of Spirits, Ming Dynasty imperial tombs (Shi [Shih] san ling, "the thirteen mausoleums"), near Nankou. (See Introduction.)

Beijing outskirts. Pagoda in the village of Balizhuang [Palichuang], 1576.

Beijing outskirts. Balizhuang. Detail of the base of the pagoda.

Beijing outskirts. Temple of the Terrace of Initiation (Jietaisi [Kieh t'ai sze]), founded 622.

Beijing outskirts. Monastery garden [Shih tze wo].

Plain of Beijing. Entrance to a cemetery. (See Introduction.)

Plain of Beijing. North Chinese traveling carts. (See Introduction.)

Plain of Beijing. Traveling carts. (See Introduction.)

Beijing outskirts. Dragon on the edge of a sluice in the Tongzhou [T'ungchou] canal.

Beijing area. Door in the Temple of the Wind God. (See Introduction.)

Pass temple on the road from Beijing to Chengde (Jehol; Rehe). (See Introduction.)

Chengde [Jehol], summer residence of the Manchu emperors. Lamaist Temple of Universal Joy (Pulesi [P'u lo sze]), 1766. Terraces and circular edifice. (See Introduction.)

Chengde. Temple of Universal Joy. Terrace. (See Introduction.)

Chengde. The former Potala (replica of the great lamasery in Lhasa, Tibet), late 1760s; view from the southeast. (See Introduction.)

Chengde. Potala. Main building. (See Introduction.)

Chengde. In a lamasery [Hingkung]. (See Introduction.)

Chengde. In the same lamasery. (See Introduction.)

Chengde. Glazed pagoda in the same lamasery. (See Introduction.)

Chengde. Gilded bronze roof in the same lamasery. (See Introduction.)

Chengde. Bridge in the imperial park. (See Introduction.)

Western Tombs (Xi ling [Siling]) of the Manchu Dynasty emperors. Main entrance. (See Introduction.)

Western Tombs. Detail of gate at main entrance. (See Introduction.)

Western Tombs. Road of Spirits in front of the entrance. (See Introduction.)

Western Tombs. Road of Spirits seen from the bridge. (See Introduction.)

Western Tombs. Bridge on the Road of Spirits. (See Introduction.)

Western Tombs. Column on the Road of Spirits. (See Introduction.)

Western Tombs. One of the grave-temples. (See Introduction.)

The Luan River (Luan he [Ho]) downstream from Chengde.

On the Luan River.

Jinan (shi) [Tsinanfu], capital of Shandong sheng. Lake of the Great Brightness (Daming [Ta Ming] hu) and the Mount of the Thousand Buddhas (Qianfo [Ts'ien fo] shan). (See Introduction.)

Jinan. Lake of the Great Brightness. (See Introduction.)

Monastery of the Magical Cliff, or Animated Summits (Lingyansi [Ling yen sze]), founded 357.

Monastery of the Magical Cliff. Buddhist cemetery. (See Introduction.)

Monastery of the Magical Cliff. Pagoda, early Song [Sung] Dynasty.

Monastery of the Magical Cliff. Statues of the forty Lohan (Buddhist apostles), executed during the Song Dynasty, in the Temple of the Thousand Buddhas.

Qingyangshu [Ts'ing yang shu], a village south of Jinan. Temple of the Tai Shan Goddess (Ming Dynasty). Hall with glazed terra-cotta reliefs.

Qingyangshu. Temple of the Tai Shan Goddess. Detail of a gable relief, showing pilgrims ascending the summit of the sacred mountain Tai shan [T'ai shan].

Tai Shan Temple (Daimiao [Tai miao]) at the foot of Tai Shan. Main entrance.

Tai Shan Temple. Main hall.

Tai Shan Temple. View of the mountain over the temple, looking north.

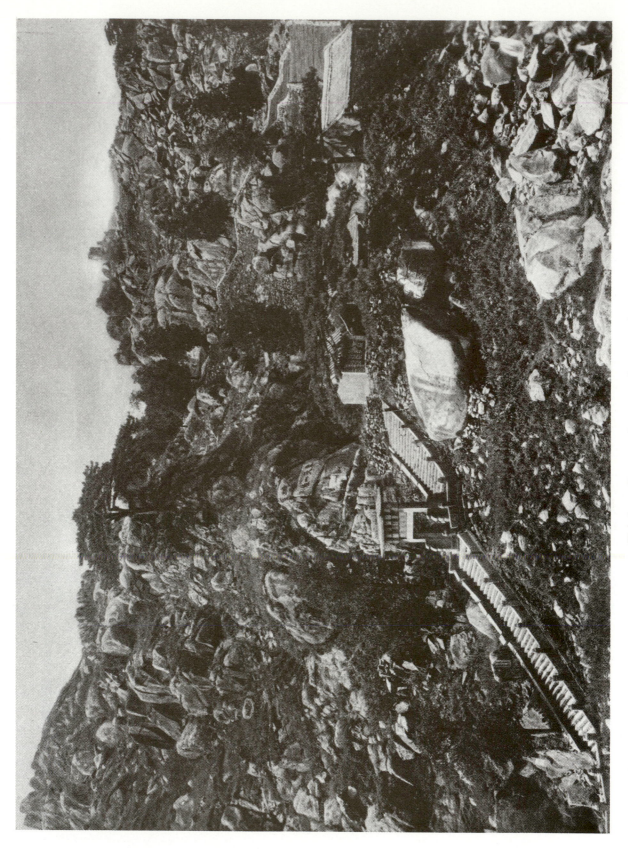

Tai shan. Stone stairway to the summit.

Tai shan. The Southern Celestial Gate (Nantianmen [Nan t'ien men]) at the summit.

Tai shan. Temple at the summit.

Qufu [K'ufu], native city of Confucius [Kong Qiu; honored as Kong Fuzi, "Teacher Kong"]. Temple of Confucius (Kongmiao [Wen miao]), main hall; marble dragon columns, ca. 1500. (See Introduction.)

Qufu. Gate on the way to the Tomb of Confucius. (See Introduction.)

Yanzhou xian [Yenchoufu]. Detail of a limestone memorial gate of the Ming Dynasty.

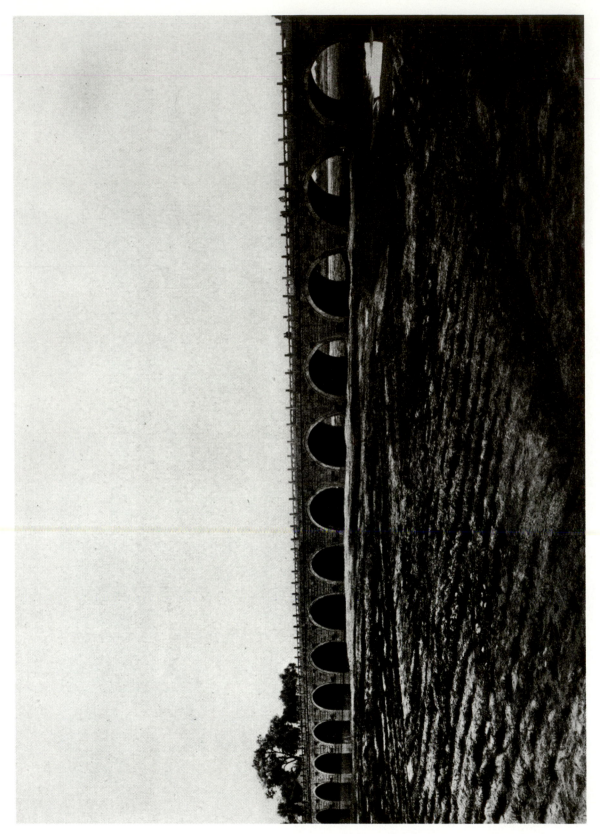

Yanzhou xian. Bridge, Ming Dynasty.

Taiyuan (shi) [T'aiyüanfu], capital of Shanxi sheng. Bronze unicorn guarding the Fen River.

Taiyuan. Temple of Great Mercy [Ta pei sze]. Thousand-armed Guanyin [Kuanyin].

Taiyuan. Temple of Great Mercy. Bronze lions at entrance.

Taiyuan. Massive hall of a temple [Shuang t'a sze].

Jinci [Kin tz'e], temple complex on the outskirts of Taiyuan. Main hall.

Jinci. Ground floor of the main hall.

Mian shan [Mien shan], a mountain range south of Taiyuan. Cave Monastery of the Cloud Summit [Yün feng sze]. (See Introduction.)

Traveling to the sacred mountain Wutai shan [Wu t'ai shan] from the north. (See Introduction.)

Traveling to Wutai shan. Ascent to the pass gate in the Great Wall. (See Introduction.)

Wutai shan (Five Summit Mountain). The Buddhist monasteries in the high valley. (See Introduction.)

Wutai shan. Monastery entrance. (See Introduction.)

Wutai shan. Painted wood carving in a monastery main hall [Shih fang t'ang]. (See Introduction.)

Wutai shan. Detail of a terra-cotta wall in the same monastery. (See Introduction.)

Wutai shan. Buddhis: library and terrace in the monastery Xiantongsi [Hien t'ung sze]. (See Introduction.)

Wutai shan. Terrace of the five gilded bronze pagodas in the same monastery. (See Introduction.)

Wutai shan. Detail of one of the above-mentioned pagodas. (See Introduction.)

Wutai shan. Another pagoda detail. (See Introduction.)

Wutai shan. Great hall of prayer in the same monastery. (See Introduction.)

Wutai shan. Great Pagoda of Sacred Relics [Shê li t'a]. (See Introduction.)

Linfen (shi) [P'ingyangfu]. Narrow defile in the loess near the city.

Linfen. Defile in loess.

Linfen. Main hall of the Emperor Yao memorial temple.

Mengcheng [Meng ch'eng]. Emperor Huangdi [Huang Ti] memorial hall.

Yuncheng xian [Luts'un], in the Jiayizhou [Kiaichou] district, native town of the 2nd-century General Guan Yu [Kuan Yü], later deified as the war god Guandi [Kuan Ti] or Laoye. The salt lake.

Yuncheng xian. Image of Guandi in his temple.

Yangwuzhen [Yang wu chen]. Residence.

Xi'an (shi) [Sianfu], capital of Shaanxi sheng. North Gate (Bei men [Pei men]).

Xi'an. North Gate. Main tower.

Xi'an. Great Mosque (Qingzhensi [Li pai sze]), founded 742. Forecourt.

Xi'an. Great Mosque. Main court.

Xi'an. Small Wild-Goose Pagoda (Xiaoyanta [Siao yen t'a]), built 706.

Xi'an. Great Wild-Goose Pagoda (Dayanta [Ta yen t'a]), originally built 652.

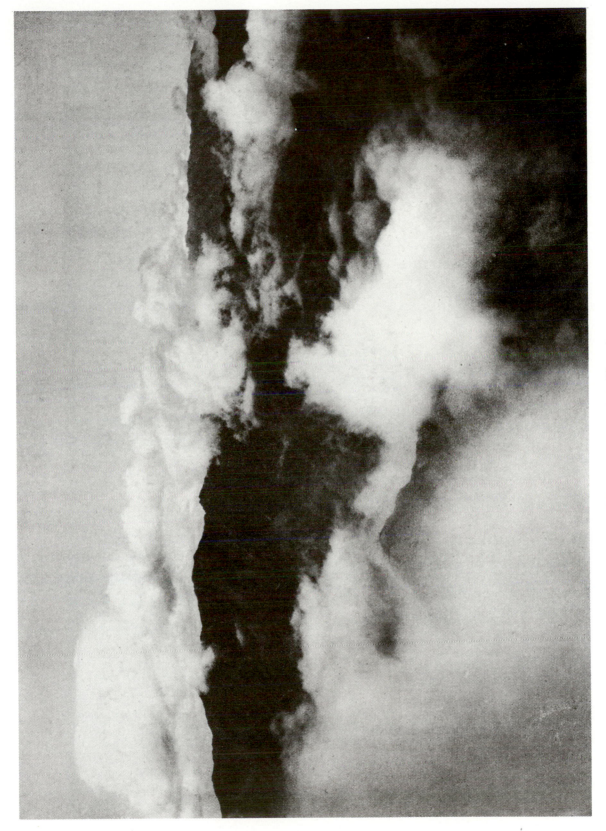

The sacred mountain Hua shan.

Hua shan. Western peak, looking north.

Hua shan. Middle and western peaks.

Hua shan. The (former) great temple (Huayinmiao) at the foot of the mountain.

Mian xian [Mienhien]. Image of Ma Chao [Ma Ch'ao] in his temple. Ma Chao, who was the comrade-in-arms of Guan Yu (see no. 90), is seen in the mural pursuing their enemy Cao Cao [Ts'ao Ts'ao].

Qinling [Ts'in ling] shan. [Miao t'ai tze.] Memorial temple of Zhang Liang [Chang Liang], chancellor to the first emperor of the Han Dynasty.

Qinling shan. [Miao t'ai tze.] Stairway to the Sacred Temple Hill.

Qinling shan [Miao t'ai tze.] Guest house in monastery garden.

Qinling shan. [Miao t'ai tze.] Monastery garden.

Qinling shan. [Miao t'ai tze.] Main court of monastery.

Qinling shan. [Miao t'ai tze.] Terra-cotta roof ridge.

Suzhou [Suchou; Soochow; Wuhsien]. Thousand-armed Guanyin [Kuanyin] of the Four Cardinal Points, in the Monastery of the Five Hundred Lohan (Jietongsi [Kieh t'ung sze]).

Shanghai. Pagoda of the Dragon Beauty Temple (Longhuata [Lung hua t'a]).

Shanghai. A silversmith's house.

Hangzhou (shi) [Hangchoufu], capital of Zhejiang sheng. The West Lake (Xi hu [Si hu]), with the ruins of the Pagoda of the Thunder Summit (or Cliff). (See Introduction.)

Hangzhou. West Lake. (See Introduction.)

Hangzhou. West Lake. Marble pagoda (18th century) in the main hall of the Monastery of the Holy Succession ([Sheng yin sze]).

Hangzhou. West Lake. Tomb of General Yue Fei [Yo Fei], unjustly executed in 1141. (See Introduction.)

Hangzhou. West Lake. Refuge of Souls Valley. The Peak That Came Flying [i.e., from India]. Rock Buddhas and pagoda.

Hangzhou. West Lake. Temple of the Forest of Clouds (Yunlinsi [Yün lin sze]; also called Lingyinsi). Pagoda.

Hangzhou. West Lake. Imperial Library [Hing kung].

Haining (xian) [Hainingchou], east of Hangzhou. Bore (tidal flood) at the mouth of the Qiantang [Ts'ien t'ang] River.

Ningbo (shi) [Ningpo; Yinhsien], major port of Zhejiang sheng. South wall of city. (See Introduction.)

Ningbo. Club of people from Fujian Province [Fukien hui kuan] in the Palace of the Celestial Queen temple. Forecourt. (See Introduction.)

Ningbo. Fujian Club. Altar of the Celestial Queen. (See Introduction.)

Ningbo. Fujian Club. Stage for theatrical performances. (See Introduction.)

Ningbo. Temple entrances.

Ningbo. Large store.

Ningbo. Large store.

Between Ningbo and Tiantongsi [T'ien t'ung sze]. On the way to the Monastery of the Celestial Boy.

Between Ningbo and Tiantongsi. Grave in the countryside. (See Introduction.)

Tiantongsi. Monastery of the Celestial Boy. Main hall. (See Introduction.)

Tiantongsi. Monastery of the Celestial Boy. Altar in the main hall. (See Introduction.)

Tiantongsi. Monastery of the Celestial Boy. The abbot. (See Introduction.)

Tiantongsi. Monastery of the Celestial Boy. Monks on their way to a service. (See Introduction.)

Putuo [P'u t'o shan], island sacred to the Buddhist deity Guanyin [Kuanyin].

Putuo. Pagoda of Prince Buddha [T'ai tze t'a], built 1334.

Putuo. Priest's grave at the summit of the mountain-island. (See Introduction.)

Putuo. Bridge to the Monastery of the Rain of Law [Fa yü sze].

Putuo. Monastery of the Rain of Law. Main court.

Putuo. Monastery of the Rain of Law. Monks' common grave. (See Introduction.)

Putuo. Monastery of the Rain of Law. Stone relief with one of the 24 classic examples of filial piety: the son whose prayers drive the Thunder God away from his mother's grave.

Putuo. Monastery of the Rain of Law. Another example of filial piety: the child who brings rice to his parents.

Putuo. Monastery of the Rain of Law. Guanyin in a white robe with green bamboo designs.

Putuo. Monastery of the Rain of Law. Marble Guanyin in a glass altar.

Putuo. Monastery of the Rain of Law. Altar of the pearl-goddess.

Yichang (shi) [Ich'angfu]. Brush Holder Mountain [Pi kia shan] opposite the cave temple of the Dragon King [Lung wang tung].

Yichang. Cave temple of the Dragon King.

Yichang. Gate hall in the Temple of the Dragon King.

Yichang. Entrance to a temple [Lingkuan tien].

Changsha (shi) [Ch'angshafu], capital of Hunan sheng. Great Temple of Confucius [Fu sheng miao], main altar. (See Introduction.)

Changsha. Ancestral temple of the Chen family [Ch'en kia tz'e t'ang]. Main court with bell tower.

Changsha. Ancestral temple of the Chen family. Bell tower.

Changsha. Memorial tablet ("spirit wall") in the temple for the 19th-century statesman Zuo Zongtang (honored as Zuo Wenxiang [Tso Wensiang]), who was born in Changsha.

Changsha. Temple of the god of literature [Wench'ang kung], main hall.

Liling [Lilinghien]. Bridge. (See Introduction.)

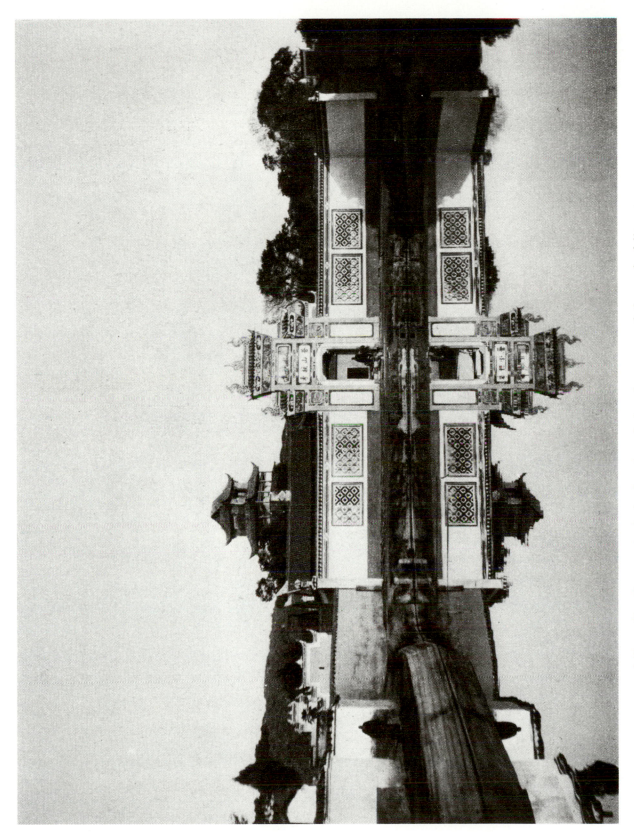

Liling. Family temple [tz'e t'ang] and the city tower of the god of literature [Wench'ang lou]. (See Introduction.)

Liling. Entrance to a memorial temple. (See Introduction.)

Liling. Memorial gates. (See Introduction.)

Heng shan, a sacred mountain also known as South Mountain (Nanyue [Nan yüo]). Main hall of the great temple at its foot (Nanyuedamiao), founded 726.

Heng shan. Nanyuedamiao. Detail of main hall.

Hengyang shi [Hengchoufu]. Temple by the Xiang Jiang [Siang River]. (See Introduction.)

Hengyang shi. Narrow street.

Lake Dongting. (Dongting [Tung t'ing] hu).

Lake Dongting. Mouth of the Xiang Jiang.

Family temple in the southern part of the province. (See Introduction.)

House entrance in the southern part of the province.

Sanduao (also Sando Ao; Sando) [Santuao; Santao]. City and harbor. (See Introduction.)

Fuzhou (shi) [Fuchou; Foochow], capital of Fujian sheng. Harbor with Drum Mountain (Gu shan [Ku shan]). (See Introduction.)

Fuzhou. Grave. (See Introduction.)

Fuzhou. Entrance to a nobleman's grave. (See Introduction.)

Fuzhou. Grave. (See Introduction.)

Fuzhou. Grave. (See Introduction.)

Fuzhou outskirts. Monastery of the Boiling Spring, or Rushing Source (Yongquansi [Yung ts'üan sze]), on Drum Mountain, founded 8th century. Prayer hall.

Fuzhou outskirts. Monastery of the Boiling Spring. Inside the prayer hall.

Fuzhou outskirts. Monastery of the Boiling Spring. Imperial double altar.

Fuzhou outskirts. Monastery of the Boiling Spring. Reclining marble Buddha in the library.

Fuzhou outskirts. Monastery of the Boiling Spring. Pagoda of relics in the library.

Fuzhou outskirts. Monastery of the Boiling Spring. State altar.

Guangzhou [Kuangchou; Canton], capital of Guangdong sheng. Great Mosque (Huaishengsi [Li pai sze]). Sacred niche.

Guangzhou. Great mosque. Interior view.

Guangzhou. Ancestral temple of the Chen family (Chenjiaci [Ch'en kia tz'e t'ang], 1840s. Street frontage. (See Introduction.)

Guangzhou. Ancestral temple of the Chen family. Side entrance. (See Introduction.)

Guangzhou. Ancestral temple of the Chen family. Main hall and altars. (See Introduction.)

Guangzhou. Temple of the god of medicine. Gable facing the street.

Guangzhou. Temple of the god of medicine. Roof ridge with dragons-and-pearl motif.

Guangzhou. Temple of the god of medicine. Reliefs in the main court.

Guangzhou. View, from the north tower, over the north city wall and the Guanyin [Kuanyin] hill. (See Introduction.)

Guangzhou. North hill (Yuexiu [Yueh siu] shan) with the tower and the temple of Guanyin; a mosque in the foreground. (See Introduction.)

Guangzhou. North hill. Sea Tamer Tower (Wucenglou [Chen hai wu tseng lou]),
standing in a line with the city wall and looking southward as religious guardian
of the city.

Guangzhou. Marble pagoda in the Monastery of the Sea Banner [Hai t'ung sze],
built in the Qianlong [Kien Lung] period (18th century).

Guangzhou outskirts. Graves in the hills north of the city. In the far distance is the White Cloud Mountain (Baiyun [Pai yün] shan); white clouds are the symbol of departed souls. (See Introduction.)

Guangzhou outskirts. White Cloud Mountain. Looking south over the numerous graves north of the city. (See Introduction.)

Guangzhou outskirts. White Cloud Mountain. Graves. (See Introduction.)

Guangzhou outskirts. White Cloud Mountain. Graves. (See Introduction.)

Guangzhou outskirts. White Cloud Mountain. Main hall of the monastery Nengrensi [Neng jen sze] on the summit; the summit is known as Moxingling [Mo sing ling], "strokes the stars."

Guangzhou outskirts. White Cloud Mountain. Nengrensi. Inner court.

Wuzhou [Wuchoufu], at the confluence of the Yu and Gui [Kuei] Rivers. Bronze
censer, 1717.

Wuzhou. Bronze censer, 1717.

Wuzhou. Memorial gate and glimpse of the Yu River (formerly West [Si] River). (See Introduction.)

Guilin (shi) [Kueilinfu], capital of Guangxi sheng. View to the east. (See introduction.)

Guilin. View to the northwest. (See Introduction.)

Guilin. An old pagoda.

Guilin. Bridge near the caves of Seven Stars Hill (Qixing [K'i sing] shan).

Guilin. Entrance to the club for people from Fuzhou [Fuchou hui kuan].

Guilin outskirts. Conical mountains north of the city.

On a journey. (See Introduction.)

Wayside grave. (See Introduction.)

Wayside altar. (See Introduction.)

Chengdu (shi) [Ch'engtufu], capital of Sichuan sheng. The octagonal hall of Laozi [Laotze] in a Taoist monastery [Ts'ing yang kung].

Chengdu. Main hall in the Wenshu (bodhisattva Manjusri) Monastery.

Village of Hanzhou [Hanchou] in the plain of Chengdu. (See Introduction.)

Roadside altar in the same village. (See Introduction.)

Luojiang [Lokianghien], in the plain of Chengdu. Waterwheel. (See Introduction.)

Shibaozhai [Shih pao chai] on the Chang Jiang (Yangzi [Yangtze]). The village, with its sacred Rock of the Ten Thousand Shadows (Wanyin shan), surmounted by a temple of the god of the underworld, reached by a staircase in a half-pagoda structure. (See Introduction.)

Chongqing [Ch'ungk'ingfu]. Narrow street. (See Introduction.)

Chongqing. House entrance on a narrow street, ornamented with glazed porcelain. (See Introduction.)

Chongqing. Cave temple dedicated to Laojun [Lao kun], the "Old Lord of the Mountains."

Chongqing. Door of a residence.

Guan xian [Kuan hien] on the Min River, nodal point of a millenary irrigation system. At the right, the temple dedicated to Li Bing [Li Ping] and his son Erlang [Örl Lang], legendary creators of the system. In the center, the (former) bamboo suspension bridge. (See Introduction.)

Guan xian. The suspension bridge. (See Introduction.)

Guan xian. The bridgehead of the suspension bridge. (See Introduction.)

Guan xian. Temple of Li Bing and Erlang. Entrance.

Guan xian. Temple of Li Bing and Erlang. First forecourt.

Guan xian. Temple of Li Bing and Erlang. Second forecourt.

Guan xian. Temple of Li Bing and Erlang. Courtyard with spirit wall.

Guan xian. Temple of Li Bing and Erlang. Main hall and incense pagoda.

Guan xian. Temple of Li Bing and Erlang. Uppermost halls.

Guan xian. Main hall in the Temple of Confucius (Wenmiao). (See Introduction.)

Guan xian. Main hall, dedicated to Li Bing, in the Temple of the Tamed Dragon [Fu lung kuan].

Guan xian. Statue of Li Bing in the Temple of the Tamed Dragon.

Guan xian. Guanyin grotto in the Soul Cliff [Ling yen sze].

Guan xian. View down the Min River toward the Qingcheng [Ts'ing ch'eng] shan mountain range.

Qingcheng shan. Cave of the Morning Sun [Chao yang tung].

Qingcheng shan. Rock chapel.

Qingcheng shan. Main hall of a monastery [San ts'ing kung].

Qingchang shan. Hall of the Celestial Queen.

Qingcheng shan. Typical scene. (See Introduction.)

Yibin (shi) [Sŭchoufu; Suifu]. View from the city up the Min River.

Yibir. A monastery [Pan pien sze] by the river.

Emei shan [O mi shan], a Buddhist sacred mountain. Pagoda of Relics in the Monastery of Ten Thousand Years (Wanniansi [Wan nien sze]). (See Introduction.)

Emei shan. The highest peak, or Golden Summit [Kin ting]. (See Introduction.)

Emei shan. Monastery buildings on the Golden Summit. (See Introduction.)

Emei shan. Mummified abbot in a monastery on the Golden Summit.
(See Introduction.)

Emei shan. The bodhisattva Puxian [P'uhien; Samantabhadra], tutelary deity of the mountain, in a monastery on the Golden Summit. (See Introduction.)

Emei shan. Hermitage of Pure Sound [Ts'ing yin ko]. (See Introduction.)

Countryside between Luzhou (shi) [Luchou] and Ziliujing [Tzeliutsing].
(See Introduction.)

Roadside altar between Luzhou and Ziliujing. (See Introduction.)

Memorial gates on the road between Luzhou and Ziliujing. (See Introduction.)

Stage in a clubhouse in Nanhuagong [Nan hua kung], a locality near Ziliujing.

Ziliujing. Salt boats in the industrial district of the salt wells. (See Introduction.)

Ziliujing. The salt-well district. (See Introduction.)

Ziliujing. Club for people from Shanxi Province [Shansi hui kuan]. Part of a room. (See Introduction.)

Ziliujing. Shanxi Club. Main court and hall. (See Introduction.)

Zilujing. Shanxi Club. Interior court with side entrance and flagstaff. (See Introduction.)

Ziliujing. Shanxi Club. Stage over the entrance. (See Introduction.)

Yuntan [Yüen t'an], a village near Ziliujing. Entrance to the temple of Emperor Yu [Yü], ornamented with glazed porcelain.

Wan xian [Wanhien]. Temple of Confucius (Wenmiao). Bell. (See Introduction.)

Wan xian. Temple of Confucius. Forecourt with pond and dragon bridge. (See Introduction.)

Wan xian. Temple of Confucius. Main hall and bell tower. (See Introduction.)

Wan xian. Entrance to the cave temple of Lord Chen [Ch'en kung tung].

Wan xian. Memorial temple of General Zhang Fei [Chang Fei], blood-brother of Guan Yu (see no. 90), with whom he conquered the old kingdom of Shu, present-day Sichuan sheng.

Wan xian. Temple of Zhang Fei. Stage for theatrical performances.

Wan xian. Temple of Zhang Fei. Porcelain roof ridge.

Wan xian. Graves and the Mountain of the Sedan-Chair Knob [Kiao ting shan]. (See Introduction.)

Wan xian. Grave on a slope of the same mountain. (See Introduction.)

Wan xian outskirts. Gate of a fortified village.

Guangyuan xian [Kuangyüanhien]. Memorial temple of the Tang [T'ang] Dynasty empress Wu Zetian [Wu Hou] by the Jialing [Kialing] River. (See Introduction.)

Guangyuan xian. Rock Buddhas above the temple of Empress Wu. (See Introduction.)

Guangyuan xian. Thousand Buddha Rock (Qianfoyan) [Ts'ien fo ai]. (See Introduction.)

Guangyuan xian. Thousand Buddha Rock. Chapel. (See Introduction.)

Qionglai xian [Kiungchou], a village near Ya'an with half-timbered houses and an incense pagoda. (See Introduction.)

王母殿

催生
送子
殿
痘母

Fengdu [Fengtuhien], formerly regarded as the entrance to the nether world. Entrance to the Temple of the Maternal Goddess [Wang mu tien].

Leshan xian [Kiatingfu]. View toward the south. (See Introduction.)

Fengjie xian [Kueichoufu] on the Chang Jiang (Yangzi). (See Introduction.)

Bellows Gorge (Fengxiang kou [Feng siang k'ou] or Fengxiang xia [Feng siang hia]) on the Chang Jiang below Fengjie. View upstream.

Bellows Gorge. View downstream.

Bellows Gorge.

Bellows Gorge.

Ya'an [Yachoufu]. View up the Ya River.

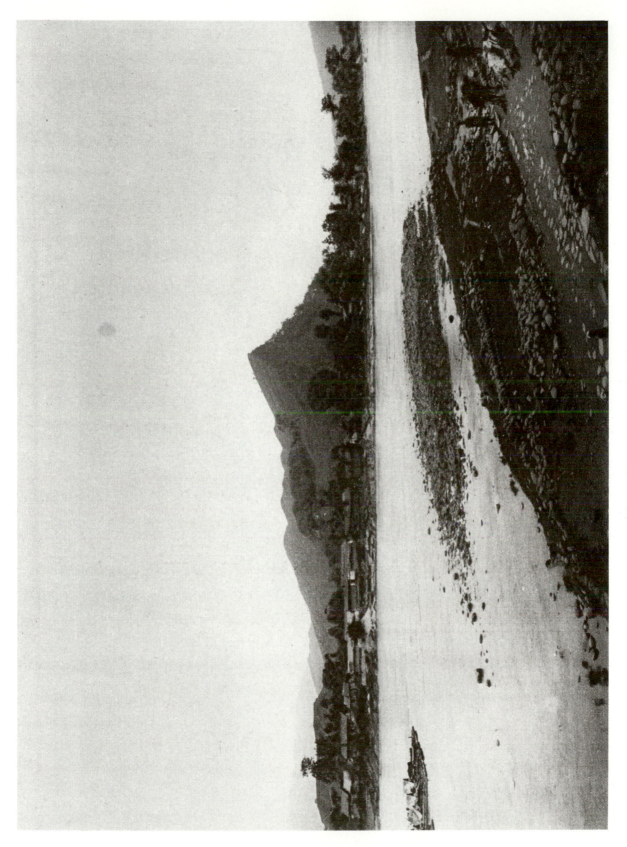

Ya'an. View down the Ya River.

Ya'an Bridge in the city. (See Introduction.)

Ya'an. Family tomb. (See Introduction.)

Ya'an. Golden Summit Monastery (Jinfengsi [Kin feng sze]). Priests' tombs. (See Introduction.)

Ya'an. Golden Summit Monastery. Tomb pagoda. (See Introduction.)